Gregory,
May you be
blessed with a long
and happy life!
love,
The Fogerty's

9/97

A Baby Blessing

A Baby Blessing

 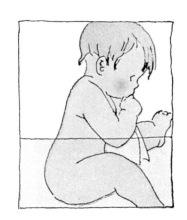 

BY WELLERAN POLTARNEES

BLUE LANTERN BOOKS • MCMXCVII

THIRD PRINTING. PRINTED IN HONG KONG THROUGH COLORCRAFT, LTD.

ISBN 1⸗883211⸗06⸗9

BLUE LANTERN BOOKS
PO BOX 4399 • SEATTLE, WASHINGTON • 98104

I here bless this baby,
newly arrived, wishing for it all the good
things I here invoke, and others beyond my
imaginings.

*May the spirits of grace attend its coming,
and may angels guide its flowering.*

3

Let this child be held and warmed ,
made secure in this strange new world.

5

*When this baby first opens its eyes,
may the face it first looks upon
be filled with love.*

 *7*

I pray that it be welcomed by many,
loved by many, and known by a myriad
of private and gentle names.

9

When this baby looks beyond
the faces of its family,
let it look upon a room where beauty reigns.
Let there be shapely toys waiting to be
touched into life, and a window
with a view of the world outside.

I wish for this child to know early in life the hugeness of trees, the cold kiss of snowflakes and the softness of rain.

THE FIRST SNOW.

*May this small life be made rich with music.
Let there be songs on waking, happy songs at
play and gentle songs at night.*

Let this baby's sleep be peaceful, and may it sail back each morning filled with the memory of sweet dreams.

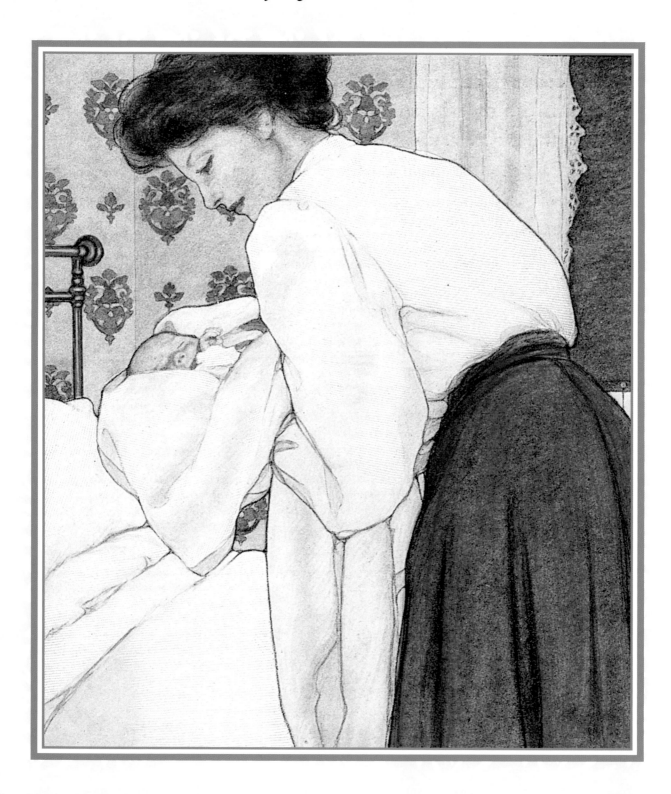

17

May play fill this young life as it blossoms, so that it may come to enjoy solitude as much as shared joy.

19

I hope that there are many animal companions, each teaching gentleness, playfulness and kinship.

May this young body grow fully, move freely, breathe deeply and see clearly.

23

I hope, as this baby grows into childhood,
that those it meets praise it freely,
encouraging its fragile mystery to bloom
into radiant self.

When this child grows up and has children
of its own, let it never forget what it was like
to be first alive and richly welcomed.

Let all those who share in this baby's growing
learn from its laughter and joy.

Picture Credits

THIS BOOK IS TYPESET IN POETICA.

BOOK & COVER DESIGN BY SACHEVERELL DARLING AT BLUE LANTERN STUDIO.

PRINTED & BOUND IN HONG KONG THROUGH COLORCRAFT, LTD.

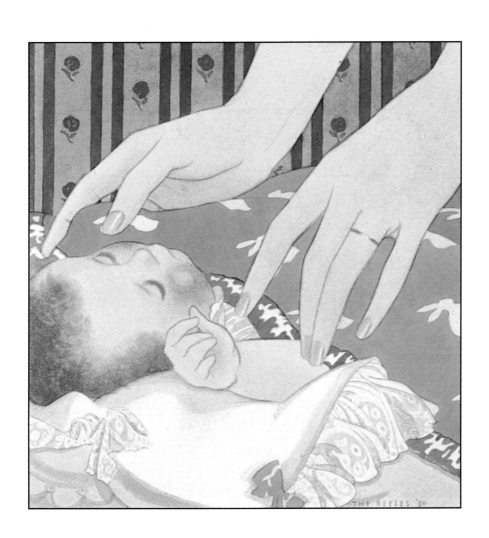

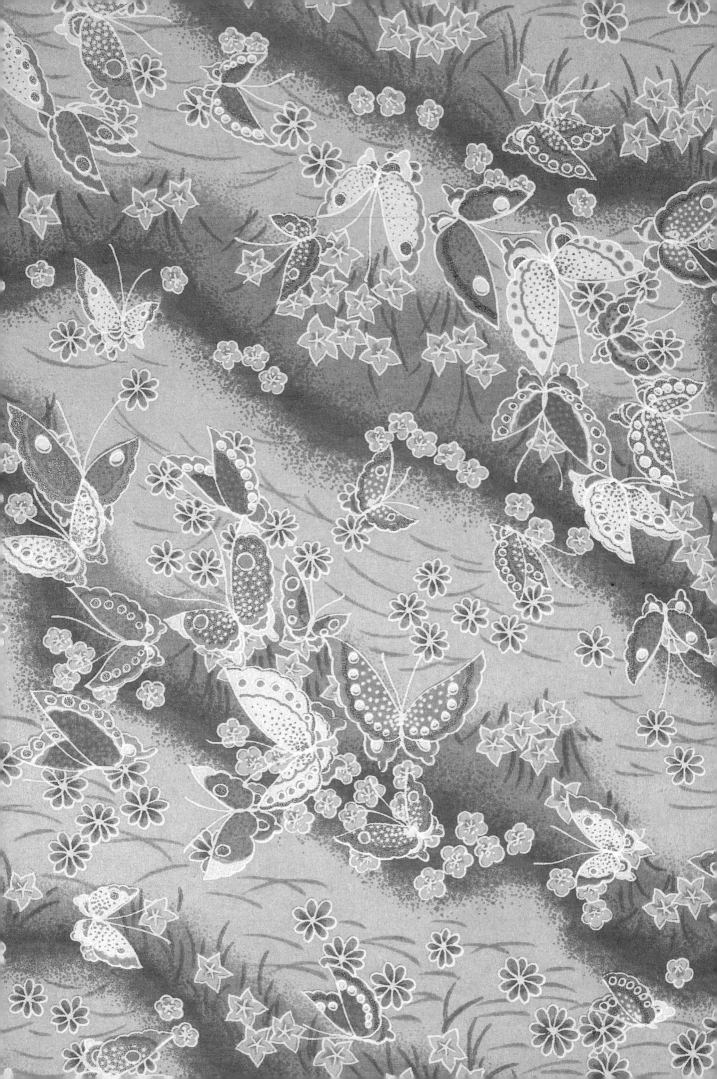